ANTENNAE

PRAISE FOR *ANTENNAE*

Nimi Wariboko's voice is a new and necessary voice in the world of poetry. In *Antennae*, he dissects the current political atmosphere of his beloved Nigeria in a critical way and to encourage positive change. James Baldwin once said that he is critical of America because he loves America. A similar thread runs through Wariboko's book, but with the face of Nigeria. The collection also has a playful touch which opens up the way to see the light that is possible when people turn from the wrong to the right. This is a must and insightful read.

— **Elvis Alves,** poet and author of *This Is What I know* (2023), *I Am No Battlefield But A Forest Of Trees Growing* (Winner, Jacopone Da Todi Poetry Prize, 2018)

In *Antennae*, Nimi Wariboko channels the pulse of Nigeria's lived experiences through simple and accessible lines, threading together personal and collective memories with an unwavering postcolonial lens. This collection is, in parts, a political pamphlet, love notes, a historical piece, a song collection, and much more. It is a testimony to the resilience of a people, where love and loss are inextricably linked to the scars of history and the weight of political realities.

— **S. Su'eddie Vershima Agema**, multiple award-winning author of *Memory and the Call of Waters* (Winner, Association of Nigerian Authors Poetry Prize 2022 and Finalist, Nigeria Prize for Literature 2022)

Antennae is an enterprising poetic offering for all-round enjoyment. Nimi Wariboko has masterfully interacted with various thematic concerns with an array of style that gives each poem in the collection a unique sensory quality.

— **Utibe Hanson**, Author of *Unnoticed Presence of Things* (Winner, Association of Nigerian Authors/KMVL Poetry Prize 2023)

Antennae is a compelling read for many reasons; not the least, for its organic connectedness. Extremely fascinating how the poems in each section add value to one another; how each section adds value to the others; and how all the poems and all the sections seamlessly build up a value-adding relationship heavy with feeling and meaning. Simply sublime.

— **Hyginus Ekwuazi,** Multiple-award winning poet and literary scholar

Antennae

Antennae articulates a musical sensibility that reveals the beauty of love, the existential horrors of politics, and the pains of death or violence within intimate circles. In lines of mystical beauty, the poems (on love, hope, and hell) probe the innermost emotions, weave together literature and political vision, and question the meaning of collective life in Nigeria. The poems are personal and social, conservative and radical, passionate and acerbic, ultimately illuminating what it means to be Nigerian. This three-part collection is redolent with politics. Not only is love viewed through a political lens, but it is also the hope that engages the hell of politics in Nigeria and yet thrives. This hope takes some of hell's fire to renew itself and aspires to use it to light the pyre of revolution.

ANTENNAE

Nimi Wariboko

noirledge

ISBN: 978-978-60717-9-4

Published in Nigeria by
Noirledge Publishing

Noirledge Publishing
Suite 223, Ogun-Oshun River Basin Development Authority,
Off Oni Memorial Children's Hospital, Ring-Road, Ibadan
Telephone: +234 809 816 4359, +234 909 666 4359
Email: hello@noirledge.com | Website: www.noirledge.com
Socials: www.linktr.ee/noirledge

Noirledge Publishing is an imprint of Noirledge Limited. For information regarding discounts on bulk purchases and special editions of our titles, please contact our Sales Department via: hello@noirledge.com or +234 809 8164 359.

Cover Design: Dhee Slyvester
Book Design: Servio Gbadamosi
Typesetting: Rukayat Amudah
Editorial Team: Utibe Hanson, Olaitan Junaid

Dedication

ix

Professor Adeshina Afolayan
for his unrelenting commitment
to bringing my poetry to various communities

Poems

Book One

Living in a Grave

The Nigerian Unborn

In the womb
the child was ready. His legs
kicked. She grimaced,
because he has no future.
So, she thought
he died
wanting to leave
Nigeria with its pains, its
wahala.
But it was late.
The doctors have come
to slap his butt
to hear him cry.
They are accursed,
as wicked, he thought, as
the politicians
who will make him
cry forever.

Burden Sharing, Nigerian Style

True Nigerians are experts at forcing
their burden on you through conversations.

As part of a tradition of
communalism or friendship,
"Happy Monday," as they
sometimes call it
they expect you to stretch out
your arm toward them
in aid, or risk having them
perish
or getting yourself
punished by God.

A whole world is thrown at you for nothing.
It is now your burden to help quickly,
the matter is urgent, more important
than your needs, complaints, sickness, life.
After all, your whole money is held in trust
for them. God blessed you because of them.

No School for Girls

*(For Grace Nwanyiaru Jack and all the girls prevented from going to school in the
1930s)*

Not that they loved schooling less
But as true patriarchy loves them more
Its care led them to utensils

They were neither dense nor opposed
To the allure of education or to reading
They loved them, these they craved
To have and to distribute
In the whole community.

Education was not a golden fleece
Fit for God's creatures of their gender
But cooking utensils set on fire
In smoking kitchens away from sight.

They said unto them, cook and wash
While the school washed away the ignorance
in their brothers' brains.

In small spaces of the kitchen
They felt their brains diminish
Into the smoke from the burning firewood.
Injustice and deprivation burnt hot blood
Into the white of their eyes.

Langston's Words for the Nigerian Market Woman[1]

She was beautiful and hardworking
and fierce like the sun
that baked her black.
And because she was desperate,
the Chief had no respect for her,
nor pity for the son in need of the money
for which she had come to him begging.

One day,
sitting on a stool in the market
measuring her onions,
She asked herself two questions:
What can a poor mother do?
with the money raised from selling in the market?
ain't there money for my son's fee?

Now the soft bed of the Chief
cared more about this poor beautiful woman;
and the slaughter room of the rich man
held a desperate mother
seeking school fees for her son.
The good community did not know this
nor cared about her.

But her only son,
Confidant of her precious innermost secret,
Knew about all her pains now
Than he ever did before,
When she sold only respectable onions.

____

[1] *Langston Hughes's poem "Ruby Brown" inspired this poem. Lines from the poem are in italics.*

Today

Two women pushing a trolley
unto the top of a rock,
an angry mother shaking her fist
at a man and then dancing.

Though I do not know why
the pushing, shaking, and dancing,
but the man turns his back slowly
and watch the trolley tear the rock
into two boulders — the living rock,
and the rock of the dead for country.
Two rocks, split selves of a country.
The first is of our new future
the other, the familiar old site
where wombs are graves swallowing
dreams, unity, faith, peace, and progress.

I do not know if the newborn
living rock will survive. Frankly,
no one is sure in this country,
Perhaps, even God. He only smiles.
God is wounded, humanity is a wound,
the nation is bleeding. Mother binds.

Many women pushing a trolley
atop a rock (moon).

Creek Road Waterside (1979)

Outside, the wind waved at the trees
This was the first sign
That the moon mocked us by its light
amid darkness.

Inside, a body prepared for mosquitoes,
sweating in the sweltering night,
 anchor to rest
Sleep is a hard sell.
I know. I lived there not long ago.
These were the other signs.

Look Down

Look down into the darkness of the grave.
Don't you see? The dust of dreams
is the terror of a country
in green colors.
Green which should
mean blossom means blistering.

Surprised by God

You have surprised us, God.
You have sent us
our full meal.

On a Lagos roadside
you made food;
our share was not
so fat as the rich's.

What is a beggar
without food?
We love you; we feel
actual joy in us,
urging us to dance.
But across, in the mansions
over the lush lawns,
a few steaks.

We think there is higher injustice:
we pray hard to you
to give us our daily bread,
heal our wounds and bind our sores
dripping with maggots
of Nigeria. Instead, you answer
the prayers of our tormentors.
God, who are you?

The rich and the poor
worship different gods.
When we watch the rich
enjoy their lives,
our hearts doubt, quiver
at the impotence of our god.

You are Next in Line

Africans, are you poor?
You are tired of being despised.
You reform every day,
Yet you lure no investor.
All you need is wisdom.
Wisdom is better reform.
China-kind of wisdom,
From poverty to riches.

You are next to grow.
My people, you are next to grow.
You are next to grow.
Receive wisdom today.
Your status is changing
from despised to honored.

Everywhere smart thinking is turning things around.
Everywhere smart thinking is turning things for you.
Everybody, come let us work together.

The Little Ijaw Drummer Boy (Christmas Song)[1]

Pa rum pum pum pum. Rum pum pum pum
Look at the people of Izon dying.
Izon children are dying from pollution.

Pa rum pum pum pum. Rum pum pum pum
And Nigerians are saying nothing.
They know but we do not matter.

Pa rum pum pum pum. Rum pum pum pum
They see but crude oil is revenue.
Citizenship in this country is vile.
And our citizenship does not count.

Pa rum pum pum pum. Rum pum pum pum)
Pa rum pum pum pum. Rum pum pum pum
Pa rum pum pum pum. Rum pum pum pum

When can we breathe air without pollution,
Or not worry about crude oil in our waters?
Pa rum pum pum pum. Rum pum pum pum

We are human beings
Created to flourish, not to perish.
We want to live, not to die.
Pa rum pum pum pum. Rum pum pum pum

Not to die
Not to die

---

[1]*A video version of this poem is available on YouTube: https://youtu.be/ZuR fsUYubQA?si=JqVgod36GG3nIvQ1*

Not to die
Pa rum pum pum pum. Rum pum pum pum
Pa rum pum pum pum. Rum pum pum pum
Fishes are now barren, can't breathe, can't eat.
Animals can't breathe, soaked in black sludge.
Pa rum pum pum pum. Rum pum pum pum

Birds dare not fly, wings leaden with crude.
Earthworms crawl as drunks, foretelling our death.
Pa rum pum pum pum. Rum pum pum pum

Trees are sick, thirsty; shrubs have shriveled.
Our land is groaning with the pain of death.
Pa rum pum pum pum. Rum pum pum pum
Pa rum pum pum pum. Rum pum pum pum

Izon is crying, Nigeria.
We want good land and justice.
We will fight for it with our life and love
No matter the odds we face.

Pa rum pum pum pum. Rum pum pum pum
We will claim our land in the barrage
Of your guns, poisoning, and suffocation.
We are determined as children
Of truth, Izon, no matter what happens,
WE WILL NOT BACK DOWN

Pa rum pum pum pum. Rum pum pum pum
Pa rum pum pum pum. Rum pum pum pum
Pa rum pum pum pum. Rum pum pum pum

God, let it happen in my lifetime.
Pa rum pum pum pum. Rum pum pum pum

Peter Obi's Youth

(After 2023 Presidential Election)

My last sorrow
is my last arrow.

It sorely pierces me raw to stow.
I shall not go

Corruption-hunting in Abuja
Nor verifying in Aso Rock or Suleja.

#ENDSARS Poem

a spectre is haunting nigeria — the spectre of endsarism
all powers of old nigeria have entered a holy alliance
to exorcise this spectre: mohammadu buhari tukur burutai
mohammed adamu babatunde fashola nigerian army, traditional media
traditional rulers religion ethnicity and regionalism.
may the patriotic youth win. wake up now and come
out swinging.

Gaza Bombing

(October 13, 2023)

Hear, O Adépòjù:
Here goes the Islamic call to prayers,
amid shelling and bombardment in dense Gaza,
it is surreal, haunting, evocative, and
speaks to the immensity of Being-Itself
that seems to ignore or is unperturbed
by the activities or sufferings of
human beings.

Hear, O Adépòjù:
The call-to-prayers seems to be saying
God supersedes all earthly reality
Does it echo the sound of the vast fecund
nothingness from which all creation emerged?
Or does the call evoke the feeling that
Being-Itself, God, is mourning, moaning in
pain as Death patrols the streets of Gaza
And Israel?

Thanksgiving

(November 23, 2023)

When the thanksgiving ends
and the guests leave our homes
it is the myth of our common soul
nourished by tours of turkey
and of our nation going to Gaza
filled by star-sprangled bombs of peace
which abides.

Morality is a Coin

Africa, you have seen now.
When you are raped, killed, tortured
maimed, beaten, spat upon
no school, university
no Harvard, MIT
no UPENN, BostonU
will say a word to save you.
Because you are poor, mean.

If you had big money
you would have forced
Harvard, UPENN, MIT, BostonU to
quake, stammer, somersault,
vomiting your millions
in their labs, banks, drawers,
kneeling, crying, sniffling.
Otherwise, you bend their necks.

Africans arise, see,
know: morality is a coin.
No one cares about you
beyond political
correctness, politeness.

Defiant Niger Deltans

For Nigerians
who grew up with toxic gas flares
like giant suns across the mangrove forest
learning what the flames and alphabets meant
for by this crude oil
this dealer of death in our community
our government hoped to develop us
For any of us
who breathed dark fumes
we were not expected to live.

And when fishermen depart we are scared
they might not bring fish
when the fishermen return we are scared
they might not sail next morning
when markets are full of foods we are scared
of deprivation
when the markets are empty we are scared
there might be famine again
when we sneeze we are sure scared
bloody black phlegm will flow
when we are deep asleep we are scared
our bodies will not be quiet
nor relaxed
and when we grin we are plain scared
our smile will be mistaken
for good life
and being alive
we are stiff scared.

So we are summoned to fight
now we are old
we were not expected to live.

America: Voices of Outsourced Centers

We bear your load as gaunt princes.
It sits in our hearts as hot spices —
This burden we endure with smiles;
While our oppressors bear no guile,
Pastors ply us with homilies.

Why should capitalists rejoice
In hiding their free market choice?
Nay, let the free world see us while
We bear your load.

We work, but, oh great America,
To you tyrant of hedonism,
They offer the aches of our souls
Daily as whips crack our skulls and soles.
As their stock markets play their roles,
We bear your load.

Born on the Wrong Side of the Sun

I was born on the wrong side of the sun
My mother and father are Africans
My home accent irritates them
So, honors, fellowships, deanships are denied me
in the American academia

Being black and African makes me unfit
For the presidency of top universities
Being black and African is damnation
In the heaven of racist academia

The sun never shines on people like me
The ship never comes in for me
The earth does not rotate with me
I must create my sun, my earth, and a new me

The Interrogation of a Nigerian Christian

Praise God, we hear
That you are a Christian
and do not give bribe. But the judges
Who pervert justice also
Do not give bribe.
You believe the Bible.
But who do you love?
You do not hate; you love all children.
You always pray.
To save who?
You are clean.
For what?
You do not fornicate or lust after others' spouses.
What impossible law do you not break?
You are a good Christian.
Are you also good with the sinners Jesus loves?

Now listen very well.
You are Christ's follower. This is why you must
Donate all your good possessions. And move
to Sambisa Forest to bring back our kidnapped girls.
In consideration of your good life, we send you
With nothing except good faith, love, and hope,
With no-tin in your good pocket with hole.

A Scared Six-Year-Old Boy in Biafra

I saw a man by the side of the boat.
His melanin stripped by Death's wet moat.
Waves bent his head into a salaam,
a posture that denies his death.
Scared, I fled as a hen without a head.

Kalabari Mothers' Pantoum for Lazy Children

When we are dead asleep, they come —
the ancestors slip into our dwelling —
inspecting rooms and kitchens,
dirty dishes annoy them.

The ancestors slip into our dwelling,
Nyíngí [mama] said to cleanse our home. But
dirty dishes annoy them. So
they send masquerades to chastise us in our dreams.

Nyíngí [mama] said to cleanse our home. But
they come to hold meetings in our dark living room.
They send masquerades to chastise us in our dreams,
to keep us busy while they talk secrets.
We run away from the masquerades, going for a big eye.
When we reached, it is our Woyíngí [Big Mama]. Her role is
to keep us busy while they talk secrets;
just before the cock crows, she lets us leave.

When we reached, it is our Woyíngí [Big Mama]. Her role is
to inspect rooms and kitchens;
just before the cock crows, she lets us leave.
When we are dead asleep, they come.

Living in a Grave

How does it feel to live in a grave?
Like a person without genitalia.
Like a being without an anus.
You drink the ocean clean, but cannot pee.
You eat for decades, but never excretes.
Your monthly periods come, but cannot exit.
You are dead, but living in a grave.
You are living, but bloated as a dead.
I am Nigeria bloated with feces.
I am Nigeria with decayed menses.
I am a country in the place of hell.
Soon my shit will hit the fan — and heaven!

Biafran-War Ijo Children (1968)

In Biafra,
class is taking a seat
at the river shore searching
and counting fresh dead bodies
believing they will rise
with the next flood tide
and the war will be over
and schools resume.

That flood tide never comes,
but the past and bodies
keep coming back to
the present, and we are
trying hard to survive.
No more waiting for our
schools to rise from the dead.

Book Two

The Antennae

A Love Supreme

There are two kinds of love:
The joy of features, which leads
to nudity in the sheets
versus the pleasures of nothingness
which find love that never fades.

The second love breeds in you what you cannot
describe, name, explain but only embrace.
Its intense awareness enters deep
inside you and flows out
creating a private world
with passion as its sun.
Concrete at first, then it becomes spirit.

But this is impossible to believe.
Something so spiritual arising from
something so concrete — *the two hearts beating
are tangible to me.* You are dead right.

Love is two hearts dying and arising together,
shedding their deadweight, born-again.
As one, they pass through walls,
disappearing in public,
floating force of pure nothingness.
Pneuma, Nephesh, Teme, Qi, they are.

Tele-Mind Conversation

Slowly she moves
bum and bum, bumbum,
then kim, kim, kimkim
they move up and down
yansh bumping against yansh.

Her blue jeans
tighten, its grips
surely weighed down
oh … oh.

You drunken bums
the pants not
Your battle ground:
Beds, sheets, couches

Hey! Listen…
Do not fall off
God knows…
finders keepers.

She moves
faster and faster
then seductively, playing
catch me if you can.

His inside swells around:
buttocks become bated clits
blue jeans turn to bedsheet
the three congested parts
meet in his loin.

        Mother!
I want to pee…
Where did the pressurized blood come from?
Why did pure blood turn to milk?

The Antennae

lascivious, extravagant, decadent
sensuous, sensational, confident
rounded, muscular, vehement
that is what they are at the moment.

Quantum Physics of Love

Your sheer unpredictability
… quirks, quarks, and sparks
　— make you a living being
　— accent the mechanics and perils of love

And your quantum-mechanical character
　— makes you breathe, vibrant
　— makes you love me
　— accents your sexual attraction

Jump as you will from particle to wave
　— you are born dual
　— you are born free
　— accentuate your dance of eros

My Love, dance for me
　draw me into your energy (àṣẹ)…
… into your divine madness
— I am already there

Your unpredictability is
— the divine madness
… of your being, love.

Intellectual High

What goal drives
the rigor of writing? A joy

that comes to others.
A joy so ecstatic, so high,
its reach
circles the readers' minds. They are

experiencing intellectual high,
elated, savoring and smiling. Then
sexual pleasure shifts, their body

captured by sensation.
Abyss: scholarship
better than sex.

And the joy
rising again. And finally
a body
glazed with ecstasy.

A Leaf Stirs

A leaf stirs in the outside field.
And suddenly ideas pour into my head,
emotions rush into my heart
as though fire has touched me.
And all my brain is primed to sizzle.

Food is sizzling on the stove; it is done.
The dining table is laid out — food
is jealous; it pushes out the ideas,
a few leaves falling from the tree outside.

Now the door opens: Boma, curvy queen, enters in her silky underwear.
For the next five minutes my
mind runs between three war-generals.

Each minute: fog of endless war.
Under each general, a weary spirit.
The flesh is strong, but the spirit is weak.

Three warring desires in one spent spirit
whose partner-flesh alone keeps
from being shredded into three parts.

The flesh is poetry, dogged and whole.
Master of desires and dreams, stirring leaves.

Love X

Love is not flesh and blood,
but the shadow, unfathomable
of flesh, blood, thought and hormones
that hallow the beloved–
the film of nothing over
the petals of their being.

I was minding my
business when the person
saw me and asked for what
I did not have. Love is some
believer in you reaching
for that part of you that
eludes you infinitely.

Some interloper, *moron*
walking into your life,
saying "I love you." What?
Then, they ask for what is
in you that is greater
than you: the sum of your
parts, endowments plus and
X, an enigma of being.

Love is the lover asking
for the mysterious something more,
the excess in you.
The intruder goes beyond
your positive properties
for the indescribable,
which is the object cause
of your lover's desire.

An Evangelist's Prayer in the Pub

Bible, do what you do best
Bring the breasts of the bride
That bare and bait in the bar
Into its holy barn.

Sugar Daddy and his Lover

Come and play with me;
why are you afraid
to knead my chest
as though its grey hairs
will turn you old?
When all they can do
is to tickle your nipples
And send you a-dieu.

Emotions

Money is sexy
sex is steamy
love is spurious
and justice
— I think
is furious–
sunshine sometimes
or a wrecking ball

The Most Beautiful Girl in Abonnema

A girl
came strutting
along the main
road,
like she was beyond
defecation,
or was
some impregnable
nun,
and if we hadn't
greeted her,
left her
alone,
We know she would've
not reckoned with
our existence, being-
there.

Christmas in Abonnema

Rice and stew all-ready
rising appetite, salivating
Christmas in Abonnema

Harmattan turns
exposed faces, hands, and legs grayish
Yuletide in Abonnema

Children in fine clothes parade the main road
and salute every adult in sight
Elders who see this idyllic setting
are so happy they give gifts to the children

Evening masquerade
exquisite and entertaining
Christmas in Abonnema

You, I — and they
entranced by culture
Christmas in Abonnema

Next year in Abonnema.

Chocolate

It is you
chocolate

far away

But roaming
inside me

you melt
into
a brown
lava
of
longing

Smithing and Bellows

Three ways of the blacksmith amaze me;
      four, I can only theologize:
the way he works with the bellows
      the way the nozzle blows air into the fire
the way of the two sacs expanding and contracting
      and the way of a phallus with a vulva.

This is the way of copulation:
    phallus bellows, blowing air in and out
      of a vulva,
    while the balls-sac claps,
    and all four say, "We are smithing creation."

Under three words, the bodies tremble
    as they utter, "Oh my God."
    as the clash of tong and labia climax
    and creation is repeated aloud.
Men and women acting divine
Blacksmith imitating, they put hammer to anvil,
    clash of metal on metal
    forging new humanity.

Our Kind of Love

We are hope calling unto hope.
Hope is the substance of our love.
And love is the form of our hope.
We are a bride and a groom grown in love.

Torment of Marriage

Like a gate
the blinds parted and
the sun looked in.
Lightly at first, then
bright moderately
until it was strong.
Then in fury it heated up.
Then in divine fury,
then at the suggestion
of any motion.

Like a day
your body opened and
his anger entered it.
A shove at first, then
dirty slaps
until he felt bold.
Then in boldness he punched.
Then in brutal boldness,
then at the emergence
of any excuse.

The good wife, when will you find
your peace? When will you
discover the safety of home?

Or do you suppose
you have no safety, since God
has not answered your prayers?

ammonia

gently
you give to me
an ancient circle
guarded by sepals

line, I lean
into its waters
stem swollen
filled with ammonia

and fall

Insight

One fortune of
gift unasked for.

From my Friend

~~In the year that King Uzziah died.~~
(*scratch, scratch it, erase it, delete*)

Selah

In the year that my mother died.
I saw also money, fluid and stacks
in my room, the scent of its power filled
the house. Above it were peace and love;
each had authority to stop abuse.

I came from the most abusive marriage,
bleakest of darkness, punched and kicked,
beaten as a dog, seared as a slave.
My putrid flesh, corpse. Hell lived with me.

In the year that my mother died.
I saw also money, fluid and stacks
And my husband was calling out to me:
"Power, Power is the Mighty Dollar
the whole house is full of its scent."

At the sight of my money, his toxic
masculinity fell out from his pouch,
the whole house is now full of peace and love.
Behold, all his habits have become new.

Selah

~~Behold, all his habits have become new.~~
(*scratch, scratch it, erase it, delete*)
Batterers do not change, they only wait.

Natality

Sombreiro River
sound asleep: no breeze
Then I alone at its bank
awakening it with my fingers
running over its sleeping face
fireflies came alive dancing
perichoretic as the gods.

Mother said: When saturated
and full of salt, Sombreiro gives
birth to mystic fireflies.
But the local sage insisted
the fireflies were the sun's sperm
mingling with the ova of the water
goddess to create new souls.
And my fingers midwifed them.

Don't Touch my Feet

Does every mother want to feel
in the morning their son's feet, warm,
to touch the sleeping flesh that
withdraws and says:
I am alive, fearful mother.
The jerk sounds to her as
Death has failed again. And God is with her.

A repetition of this every day
because it was impossible for mama
to forget so quickly her three losses.

Nobody Knows her Troubles

The monster of man lives
in my friend's home,
only my friend sees him. She and her husband
share a room in the home.

She works hard to feed him
clothe him, sex him. The man
beats her, branding her with hot
iron on her butt. Yet she strokes
his body, cares for him as she would God.
Daily, she grinds,
indifferent to slaps.

Nothing changes for her.
Hard work, hot slap, hot prayer,
Hard work, hot slap, hot prayer,
Hard work, hot slap, hot prayer…

Nothing is any different.
Even the image of the iron and
God is the same yesterday, today and forever.
Nothing changes in my friend's room.

The Day Mother was Buried

At the end of her love and life
She was buried.

Listen to me: that which you call grave.
I remember.

Preacher, words, sounds of dirt falling on casket
Then darkness. The walk back
leading thoughts into dry wells.

It is scary to meditate
on flesh and blood
living in the dark earth.

Now a consciousness: that which you love, being
disembodied, unable
to hug, displaced forever, the old self
salting the earth. And what I hear to be
voices talking in low tones.

Those who cannot understand
conversations of consciousness
I tell you do not love: whatever
is buried returns as power
to give message:
from my mother, the new power,
a great WhatsApp voicemail.
God is talking to me now.

The Suffocation

My soul drenched.
Like the remains of a wrecked ship
washed atop the sea. Waterboarded,
it struggles. Soggy,
not from absorption, but from violence,
the aftermath of wedding.

Brain, summoned to leave the skull,
To walk unhinged for a moment,
disconnected, as before
from reason and logic of existence —
woman gamed out of sagehood
by the promise of marriage,
how will she ever again accept
the values of society?

My soul soaked and widened.
Our society became for it too suffocating.

And when my brain returned to me
I was another woman absolutely.

The Big Man's Wife

Once she could imagine her life,
She could imagine her marriage.
When she imagined her marriage,
her life dried. This,
every nice girl knows too well.

The rest, her husband already knows.
A few moments of joy, then
the dense shadow, like the darkness in the womb,
before the knuckles send her
brain back to the reptilian state.

The etiolated brain is her machine
of respectable marriage.
And her brave brain and soul have long died.

But her body perdures.
Not living, but perduring.
Do not ask me why.

But her soul asks: *oh, my body
why did you leave me?*
Silence.

The Lady Named Gold

Her movement was graceful,
almost balletic in form,
slim feet touching the ground
with feminine sweetness.

Now after childbirth,
a tormentous marriage,
thirty-three odd years spent
living in three continents,
she is still …
amazingly light in strides.

From scalp to sole, one sauce (source)
of good and true beauty.
Did one ever see a more
beautiful ballerina?

Falola's Burden at 71

(for all African scholars)

I am trying to bear witness
To African ingenuity
In my scholarship. And I aim
To do it so brilliantly that
When I am long dead, future
Africans — all scholars — who search
For evidence of black excellence
Or witness or first-class thinking
In a past period will be able
To find my work beneath the pile
Of debris of history and time.
And history will come alive
For them. The past will not perish.
I am not dead, oh Africa!

Falola's Joke at 71

Falola,
Any writer can laugh when his book comes out,
And it's all put on many bookshelves.
But the writer who's learned
Is the writer who can laugh
When his book's put on many brain-shelves.

Falola,
Any writer can laugh when his book comes out,

Bele at 30

Bele,
born between
wisdom and favor
sandwiched as a Christian
dwelling between Sophia and Grace.
May God shed his grace on thee
And crown thy beauty with good
From time to the end of it.

History and Time

Mehn, History and Time are not buddies.
History is the s(t)age of time.
Time is the s(t)age's fourth dimension,
invisible, abstract, asymptotic.
Where they blur is trauma of the present.
Where they depart, History lies.
Where they fall in love, History is trapped.
Where they fight, History becomes meaningless.
For Time and History
do not know how to live together:
History mocks Time,
and tale and tale and tale again
History traces Time in senseless motions.

The Dream of Amos Tutuola

I saw a bird with lovely tongue stud.
I am a tree: flowers, petals, stigma.
Tongue on petals lifted my stigma
And the bird shifted pollen into it.
Like the woman in Benini's sculpture
I was enraptured, ecstatic, pierced.

Oh, my fingernails dug deep into
My bedside table, clawing its surface.
As an oil-bean pod in my head exploded
   startling the forest
   scattering its birds
   shaking me out of myself.
I changed myself into an oil-bean tree
Trunk moving, dancing, pods exploding.

<u>*Book Three*</u>

Hope Lives in Hell

Abonnema Evacuation

(Biafra War, June 21, 1968)

The sadness in their faces at the waterside:
Fishes on a dry, sand beach.

The Day of the Lord

On the last day
the earth will
not end by fire
not even water
but by salt
sprinkled on
pure polluters
to wriggle in as
earthworms

God and Aso Rock

Yesterday
I saw flies
take selfies
with two crows
on the brows
of God's face.

Out of tick — why did God
allow it — "because He
loves flies, crows, and selfies."

Today
I saw girls
cry, crying
in thousands
at the Aso Rock
of richness.

Out of shit — what is their
problem — "our president
loves lies, cries, and sorrows."

the man, alone

you wonder why I am a man
and live in a woman-less
house located in a
posh neighborhood
without children.

you wonder why
I am an old Nigerian
man of lost hope
expecting 'morrow
from a ruined past.

I am the not-yet African
awaiting birth
by a girl.
I am tomorrow
wedged in the birth canal.

pull me out
today.

Inaugural Day Wisdom

The President shouts "Remove,"
The Minister shouts "Subsidy,"
The economist shouts "Petrol subsidy ruins our economy,"
A General Overseer says, "God's President."

A sick child on the surgery table just died from lack of power
As the hospital had no fuel in its generator.
A Wall Street banker called that some data.

Now here's is a live portrait… *Crude price up and naira down.*

It's incompetence as usual.
Power grid down.
Poverty kills the poor
And politicians don't care.

Now here is a live portrait…

One beautiful woman
Super-curvy shape
With
Brazilian wig
British accent
Sexually provocative skirt,
And a spiritually modified hustle.

It's education mishap,
It's incompetence as usual.

Telephone Conversation with Aso Rock[1]

The call seemed endurable, wahala
Understandable. The President swore he ruled
Excellently. Nothing mattered now
But introduction. "Sir, I am serious,
I hate black people — I am white, racist."
Excitement. Excited readiness of
Africanized fawning. Mouth, when it spoke,
Foully tongued, corruption-laced
Patriotism-emptied. Happy I was.
"HOW MANY?" … Did I hear wrong?…" PROSTITUTES
OR SLAVES?" Hello Sir, Hello Ma. Fu*k
Cold winter wind of New York City
Snow, ambulance noise, crowded streets.
It was real! The president said it.
Surprised by his savviness, surrender.
Not ashamed to beg clarification.
Professional he was, rephrasing himself,
"DO YOU WANT YANSH? OR MEN?" Truthfulness came.
"You mean you are exchanging Nigerians for money?"
His response was quick, brilliant in its simplicity,
Businesslike, skilled, market-oriented.
I offered: "Strong young men, ten-dollar per person.
Five extra per person for you." Excitement for positive
Cash flow till revelation changed his mood.
Assuming vexatious voice, "WHAT DID YOU SAY?"
"I said, 'I am a Nigerian journalist.'"
"SHUT UP BEFORE DSS CATCH YOU."
"Ole, you be thief."

---

[1]*This poem was inspired by Wole Soyinka's "Telephone Conversation."*

"I NO BE THIEF"
"You be rogue."
"I NO BE ROGUE"
"You be armed robber."
"GOD PUNISH YOU FOR PRANKING ME."
"You no want dollar again."
"Yeye president."

A Little Child is Born

In Lagos and Kano
In Awka and Yola
A little child is born
Mother is weary
Father pacing in agony
Neighbors are living in poverty
All analysts of Nigeria agree,
President is dead
President is dead.
In Lagos and Kano
In Awka and Yola
Christians are twice born
Muslims are salaaming weary
Traditionalists are cursing in agony
Neighbors are dying in poverty
And the citizens all agree,
Long live corruption
Long live corruption.

The World is a Child

God made woman a still
The man a distiller.
One of them is rich — *Poros.*
The other is poor — *Penia.*
Together, they birthed
Eros, spirit of the world.
The world is whiskey. It either
Makes humans very rich
Or renders them very poor.

Now a Professor

When I was a student reading
my professors' books, you know
what I felt? I felt brilliant.
Now that I think for myself,
pathbreaking, but also pointless.
Also very ambitious.

The Hawk and the Chick

The hawk lifted the chick
with its claws,
its dry-season fare.

The chick cried aloud.
Then it said to the hawk
I am not crying because
I want you to let go
of me. But someone should
inform my owner, the
old woman, from whence comes
my death.

Chicks do send messages home.
Someone should discuss with God
where Nigerians should send
their messages as their leaders
tear into their raw flesh.

Hope Lives in Hell

Hope is to be scared of death
and walk toward hell.
Courage is to stand in hell
until life fires death.

Then take some hell's fire
to light your own pyre
of rage against hate.

Rain Rushing to the River

The rain
ruins roofs
of our thatch houses
then it rushes
off to die in the rivers

Short Speech

It is only a short speech,
and it took little time to write,
but like a striking force
it scattered our foes
and made the vote worth
righting.

Image of Satan

Each generation must, out of its troubled
Imagination and conscience, discover
Satan awake or proclaim him asleep
in the generation before it.

Each African Pentecostal must look
under their village stone to discover
the ancestral "curse" their pastor kept there,
reject it or disown the fake pastor.

Nigeria must, out of its relative
darkness of demons and fake pastors, know
the God-beyond God that lets all light down
or the God that lets all the darkness down.

The Green Rain

Tonye paints green
rain

on a white
canvas

full of black fruit
trees

holding three red
bird nests

Monster as Leader

His brain is fish scales
His heart is pig
His navel is vulva
His penis is goat
His governance is Golgotha.

Her blood is whiskey
Her breast is bribery
Her brain is camel-toe
Her back is steel
Her governance is Gethsemane.

Combine his brain and hers
--- dark waters of dead fishes

Her blood and his heart?
--- the Devil's sperm

His navel and her rear?
--- the Devil's anus.

What is this monster?
A Nigerian Politician!

Man and his Balls

He talked of Abuja
Dubai, DC, Doha —
This man of the big bank
With the biggest in money and balls!

"You are rich and powerful, Man."
"Thank you," he said and then
"The bank gorges with billions."
   I said sai.
"The money in dollars."
"The balls on heat."
   I said baba.

"You are not listening!" he screamed,
 Slapping my face turned elsewhere at breasts,
A lady's breasts with a cancerous lesion
And her face sulked sad with fear
Then slowly she comes closer, salaaming at his rear
To stretch forth her hands — handsome and brave,
Breaking the balls of the charlatan.

Ouch!

Lady with Roses

Lady,
plunged her word into his stomach — twisted it.
Then she put roses on his head.
"This is how to nicely reject a man,"
She said.

Kalabari Princess in India

Kali kulu kulu Kalika
Ogborigbo Ogborigbo
The drum name of a Kalabari
king, not Hindu goddess.

Kali kulu kulu Kalika
Dum/da, da/da, da/da, **Dum**/da/**Dum**
Ogborigbo Ogborigbo
Dum/da/**Dum**, **Dum**/da/**Dum**.

Indians even borrowed my **name** nimi.
Nepalese Nepalese,
Nimi was their dead **king**.
Japanese **Japanese**,
Love nimi **Love** nimi

India, Nepal, Japan
Stop pretending you do not know us
Kalabari gave you Kalika.
underdevelopment destroyer,
Kalabari daughter.
We sent her a teacher;
You made her a goddess.

When you did not return her to him,
Her father, the king, cried, he cried:
Kali kulu kulu Kalika
Kulu: retreat, enfold your powers.
Kulu: the water that removes evil.
Ogborigbo: gather her energy.
Ogborigbo: gather our energy.

Today, in remembrance of his cry
Kalabari males during funerals
tie a well-folded cloth on their heads,
named *ogborigbo*. And the drums beat:

Kali kulu kulu Kalika
Ogborigbo Ogborigbo

Metal on Concrete

"Metal on concrete jars my drink lobes."
Soyinka, too cerebral.

"A running splash of rust and gold."
Clark, too idyllic for today.

"At dawn slowly the sun withdraws."
Achebe, thought too personal.

"Metal on cranium jets
A running splash of blood and lobe
As God slowly withdraws
His arms of protection
When the people who created power
Awoke and stormed Aso Rock."

Who wrote this scary poem?

In Love: You and Kafka and Paul

You hate more than you love.
You hate this, you hate that.
Often, I don't know what
I am guilty of. Love
warmth, sincerity, what?
Loving you is like living
in a Kafka novel.

Loving you is like reading
Saint Paul's Romans seven
verse seven: "Thou shall not
covet." Covet what, Paul?
"I don't know. Don't covet!"
This is unfair. Moses
in his Exodus twenty
seventeen was clear about
what not to covet. But
you Paul is the creator
of Kafka characters.

Nimi Wariboko is a public intellectual and the Walter G. Muelder Professor of Social Ethics at Boston University. He is the author of *Kálábárí Témétéín Ékwen (Kalabari Poems)*. He is also the author of *Social Ethics and Governance in Contemporary African Writing: Literature, Philosophy, and the Nigerian World* (2023).